DECREE IT AND LET GOD MANIFEST IT

30 DECLARATIONS TO SPEAK OVER YOUR LIFE

YOLANDA MARSHALL NICKERSON

Copyright ©2019 by Yol and Marshall Nickerson

Published by Olympus High Glory Christian
Book Publishing
ISBN 978-0-9983588-3-3

Printed in the United States of America

Unless otherwise identified, all Scripture quotations in this publication are from the NIV version and the New King James Version

All rights reserved. No part of this publication may be reproduced, stored in a retrieval system, or transmitted in any form or by any means of electronic, mechanical, photocopied, or otherwise, without the prior permission.

CONTENTS

DECREE IT AND LET GOD MANIFEST IT

What are you speaking over your life? Are you speaking positively or negatively about yourself and your situations? Did you know that your words have power? Did you know that "life and death" are both in the power of your tongue? Did you know that you can decree and declare some things (good or bad) in and over the course of your life and they will manifest?

It is quite easy for any of us to choose words to speak according to how we are feeling. Many of us are

9

moved by our emotions; therefore, when things are not going so good for us or when things have not happened as quickly as we would like for them to, we tend to speak negative words. When we speak negative words, we not only give our adversary the opportunity to have control over our situations, but we also see negative things manifest in our lives. Negative speaking yields negative results and positive speaking yields positive results. You don't have to continue speaking negative words. You can actually change the way you speak. You can start speaking in a positive way about any situation in your life. And you can start right *now*.

As you read this book, you will find thirty declarations that you can speak over your life, along with an area for you to write down any special requests to God that pertains to any of those declarations. I want you to know that Heaven has the capacity to release to you whatever it is that you need or desire. You must also believe that "God can do anything but fail." So, go ahead and decree it and let God manifest it.

12

DAY ONE

I DECREE THAT I WILL HAVE WHAT GOD PROMISED ME

"Thou shalt also decree a thing, and it shall be established unto thee: and the light shall shine upon thy ways."
Job 22:28

I want to let you know that whatever God has promised you, He is going to fulfill that promise. Just because you have not seen the promise manifest in your life yet, it does not mean that it is not going to happen for you. "For all the promises of God in Him are yes, and in Him amen..." (2 Corinthians 1:20-NKJV).

13

He does not ever make a promise that He cannot keep.

Sometimes God will allow the promise to be delayed because He is trying to rid you from something so that you can be ready to receive the promise. He could also be trying to detach you from some people who are not a part of the promise. One thing that you have to remember is that if something is delayed, it does not mean it will be denied.

Every now and again, you may need to have a conversation with God and remind Him of what He promised you—marriage, a new home, a new vehicle, a job promotion, a business, a ministry, or something else. After you remind Him of what He told you, He is going to whisper in your ear, "I am still going to do it for you. I am still going to fulfill what I promised you."

I want to let you know that you are in your "set up now" season. It is God who has set you up and it is He who is going to manifest what He promised you in this season of your life. There are some things that He has set aside just for you, and it is His will and desire to give you these things. You are about to enjoy wrapping your arms around every single thing that He's promised you.

DAY TWO

I DECREE THAT I WILL RECOVER ALL

"Thou shalt also decree a thing, and it shall be
established unto thee: and the light shall
shine upon thy ways."
Job 22:28

It is not easy to cope with losing anything. It is not uncommon to feel sad, depressed, disappointed, or angry after losing something. You may have lost time in an abusive relationship or even on a job that did not value your worth. You may have lost a lot of tangible things. You may have lost a house. You may have lost a vehicle.

17

You may have even lost your peace and your joy, due to losing something.

I remember when I was in grad school at Troy University many years ago, I lost my apartment due to being evicted, my car was repossessed due to financial lack, and I nearly lost my mind. That was a very trying season for me. But just as I remember losing those things, I remember when God restored those things and much more.

I want to let you know that God is fully capable of restoring anything that you lost, too, and I believe that He finds joy in doing that for you. He declares in His Word that He will restore to you the years that the locust hath eaten, the cankerworm, and the

caterpillar, and the palmerworm...
(Joel 2:25).

God also specializes in giving back double, even triple. So, whatever it is that you need to recover, get ready to receive it back. Have faith that you will receive it back. Believe that you will receive it back. And do not be surprised if you receive double or triple.

DAY THREE

I DECREE THAT I WILL BE WEALTHY

"Thou shalt also decree a thing, and it shall be established unto thee: and the light shall shine upon thy ways."
Job 22:28

You have the power to obtain wealth. That's right! Did you know that God gave you this power the moment you were born? Wow! Isn't that amazing? His Word says, "...For it is He who gives you power to get wealth." (Deuteronomy 8:18-ESV). That Scripture is your assurance that you have all that you need to become wealthy.

21

Your gifts and talents, coupled with your desire to become wealthy, will cause doors to open for you when you least expect it, propelling you to that wealthy place. If you want to start that business, do it. If you want to write a book, do it. If you want to become a model, do it. If you want to create an invention and turn it into a product, do it. Remember, again, "You have the power to get wealth." Do not let anyone tell you differently. Surround yourself with positive people who believe in you, who will give you a spiritual push you, who will support you, who will help you give birth to all that is within you, and who want to see you become wealthy. The Word of God says that "A man's gifts

22

makes room for him and brings him before great men." (Proverbs 18:16). It is about time for this Scripture to work in your favor, so get ready to take your seat at the table with some distinguished people.

DAY FOUR

I DECREE THAT I WILL PROSPER

"Thou shalt also decree a thing, and it shall be established unto thee: and the light shall shine upon thy ways."
Job 22:28

It is the will of our Heavenly Father that you prosper. "Beloved, I wish above all things that thou mayest prosper…" (3 John 2:2). Let this Scripture serve as your motivation to position yourself to prosper.

It is time for you to start from the bottom and go to the top. It is time for you to move from the back of the line to the front of the line. It is time for you to stop settling for less. It is time

25

for you to come from that place of scarcity. It is time for you to stop living from paycheck to paycheck. It is time for you to receive an increase in every area of your life. It is time for you to live out your dreams. God wants you to have all that He has in store for you.

DAY FIVE

I DECREE THAT I WILL BE SUCCESSFUL

"Thou shalt also decree a thing, and it shall be established unto thee: and the light shall shine upon thy ways."
Job 22:28

You have to believe that you will be successful, and you have to know that God wants you to succeed. With the wisdom of God and His leading, you will succeed in whatever you put your mind to, and you will always end up in the right place at the right time. His Word declares, "The steps of a good man are ordered by the Lord." (Psalm 37:23).

When you take those steps, as He leads, you will be able to seize every opportunity He presents to you. You will be able to easily eliminate the fear of failing, because you will know that God is with you, and guiding your footsteps. There is a place for you in the world of success.

DAY SIX

I DECREE THAT I WILL WALK IN MY PURPOSE

"Thou shalt also decree a thing, and it shall be
established unto thee: and the light shall
shine upon thy ways."
Job 22:28

Do you know what your purpose is? Have you been limiting yourself? Is there anything that you find joy in doing, and are very passionate about doing? Pastor Rick Warren said it best in his book Purpose Driven Life, "Passion produces purpose." Those words were an eye-opener for me. I learned of the things that I was so passionate about doing and I started

29

carrying out my purpose. I want you to know that you are purposed to do great things as well. You are still full of life; that means you still have work to do. You still have some places to go. You still have some minds to change. You still have some people who need your influence. You still have a God to glorify in all that you do.

God has filled you with so many wonderful gifts and talents; these two things will aid you in carrying out your purpose. God will also be there to cover you and walk alongside you as you do what He has purposed you to do. He is your biggest cheerleader in the Spirit.

DAY SEVEN

I DECREE THAT I WILL WALK IN POWER

"Thou shalt also decree a thing, and it shall be established unto thee: and the light shall shine upon thy ways."
Job 22:28

Do you realize how much power you possess? You have power to command things to come into proper alignment in your life. You have power to speak life over every dead thing that needs to be resurrected in your life. You have power to get wealth. God declares in His Word that He's even given you power to tread over serpents. (Luke 10:19). Start using the power that God has given

31

you and stop allowing the devil and the people he is using to intimidate you.

There is no need to be intimidated by someone else's power. You should be confident in walking in the power that God has given you as a child of His. The same greater is He that is in them, is the same greater is He that is in you. When you tap into this truth of His Word, you will walk freely in power for the remainder of your life. I must also let you know that He has given His angels charge over you. (Psalm 91:11). That is all the more reason to use your power.

DAY EIGHT

I DECREE THAT I WILL HAVE THE JOY OF THE LORD

"Thou shalt also decree a thing, and it shall be
established unto thee: and the light shall
shine upon thy ways."
Job 22:28

The joy of the Lord is something you must desire to have in your possession every single day. God is the source of joy and He wants you to have it forever. The joy of the Lord will keep your spirit lifted when you are dealing with chaos in your home or anywhere else.

In order to remain full of joy, you cannot allow anything to creep in and

33

steal it. You must speak to any evil spirit that may try to steal your joy and tell it that there is no room in your life for it. Be mindful that your adversary does not want you to ever experience joy, so he will use anyone or anything to steal it. He seeks to rob you of your joy as often as he can. Do not allow that devil to steal it another day. Start commanding your day the moment you open your eyes every morning by saying, "This is the day that the Lord has made; I will rejoice and be glad in it." (Psalm 118:24).

DAY NINE

I DECREE THAT I WILL HAVE PEACE

"Thou shalt also decree a thing, and it shall be
established unto thee: and the light shall
shine upon thy ways."
Job 22:28

It is not uncommon to have many things on your mind at the very same time. However, you must learn how to control what enters your mind. You should not entertain anything negative that comes to occupy space in your mind and rob you of your peace.

There is nothing like having true peace in your life. I want you to know that you can have peace in whatever situation you will ever face, even the

35

one that you may be dealing with at this moment. You do not have to surrender to any situation that is intended to steal your peace. You do not have to surrender to the spirit of confusion. You do not have to agree with confusion nor allow it to enter and contaminate your mind, altering your positive thoughts.

God wants you to "have peace that surpasses understanding" so that you can continue focusing on positive, wholesome, uplifting things in life. Philippians 4:8 says, "...whatever is true, whatever is honorable, whatever is just, whatever is commendable, if there is any excellence, if there is anything worthy of praise, think about these things.

DAY TEN

I DECREE THAT I WILL HAVE FAITH

"Thou shalt also decree a thing, and it shall be established unto thee: and the light shall shine upon thy ways."
Job 22:28

Sometimes things will happen to minimize your faith. If your faith is not solid, you will find yourself doubting God time after time. In order to get God to move for you in any situation that you will ever encounter in life, you want to make sure you have at least the faith that is the size of a mustard seed. Read Matthew 17:20.

When you have doubt and fear, you limit God from responding to your situation. It is almost like you tie the hands of God when you walk in doubt and fear. He wants to see your faith in action. "Without faith it's impossible to please God." (Hebrews 11:6).

I want to encourage your faith by directing you to read more Scriptures about faith. The more you get those Scriptures in your spirit, the more you have to stand on. The more your faith is increased, the more you will believe God, and the more you will see Him do for you. "…According to your faith, be it unto you." (Matthew 9:29).

DAY ELEVEN

I DECREE THAT I WILL HAVE A CONSISTENT PRAYER LIFE

"Thou shalt also decree a thing, and it shall be
established unto thee: and the light shall
shine upon thy ways."
Job 22:28

When you pray, it is a way to communicate to God. When you have a relationship with Him, you should want to communicate with Him every single day. Therefore, it is necessary to have a consistent prayer life. The Bible tells us to "Pray without ceasing" in Thessalonians 5:17. That means nonstop. You cannot afford to have any gaps in your prayer life, especially with all that is going on in our world today.

You may even have some difficult things going on in your personal life right now that you need to pray about. You should pray about that which concerns you until you see change, because "Prayer changes things." I want you to know that you should not only pray when things are difficult in your life. You still need to pray when things are going well, too.

If you do not have a consistent prayer life, I encourage you to ask God to help you to develop one. Ask Him to give you the desire to pray more, even when you do not feel like it. Ask Him to give you a praying spirit. "Ask and it will be given to

40

you…" (Matthew 7:7-NIV). He will take your prayer life to another level.

DAY TWELVE

I DECREE THAT I WILL STAY FOCUSED

"Thou shalt also decree a thing, and it shall be
established unto thee: and the light shall
shine upon thy ways."
Job 22:28

It is important that you stay focused in this season of your life so that you can be more productive than you have ever been and achieve the goals that you have set for yourself. If you are not focused, you will find yourself being behind schedule on a lot of things that you desire and aspire to do, and you do not want that to happen.

You must understand that your adversary will do whatever he can to direct your attention on other things that are not important. He will bring one distraction after another, just to take you off course and stop your progress. You cannot allow yourself to continue being distracted. You have to find ways to eliminate distractions. Your mind has to be clear of all distractions so that you can stay focused on your goals, and anything else that matters to you.

DAY THIRTEEN

I DECREE THAT I WILL BE BLESSED WITH IT

"Thou shalt also decree a thing, and it shall be established unto thee: and the light shall shine upon thy ways."
Job 22:28

There may be one particular thing that you really need God to bless you with. You may need it right *now*. Whatever *it* is that you need Him to bless you with; whether that need is spiritually or naturally—I want you to know that He can easily bless you with that thing.

It is nothing for Him to bless you with having peace of mind, a joyful heart, strength to move beyond your

45

current situation, or the money you need to pay an overdue bill, the transportation you need to get from one destination to the next, the apartment or house you need for you and your family, the proper clothing to wear to that job interview, work, etc. Ephesians 3:20 says, "Now unto him that is able to do exceeding abundantly above all that we ask or think, according to the power that worketh in us."

DAY FOURTEEN

I DECREE THAT I WILL HAVE VICTORY OVER IT

"Thou shalt also decree a thing, and it shall be
established unto thee: and the light shall
shine upon thy ways."
Job 22:28

You may have been weakened by
something that happened in your life.
You may have gotten a bit angry
because things appear not to be
working out for you. You may have
literally buried your head in your lap
because the trial you are now facing
seems to be lasting longer than the
previous one. You may be trying to
figure out how you are going to win
this time around.

47

You can rest in the Lord and be assured that you will no longer be on the losing end of the spectrum. In this season of your life, "You will win, and everything attached to you will win." (Jekalyn Carr). You can have total victory over anything that is determined to defeat you.

DAY FIFTEEN

I DECREE THAT I WILL MAKE IT THROUGH THIS STORM

"Thou shalt also decree a thing, and it shall be established unto thee: and the light shall shine upon thy ways."
Job 22:28

Over the years, we have heard about so many natural storms that caused major destruction across the United States, and beyond. While natural storms are usually forecasted by meteorologists, we also encounter storms of life that God will allow our spiritual leaders to warn us about or He will reveal it to some of us in dreams, whether it be a storm in our finances, in our relationship, in our

49

health or another area of our life. Oftentimes the hard part is weathering the storms that you encounter as an individual, but the best part is knowing that you are not alone in a storm. God is with you. He said in Hebrews 13:5, "I will never leave you, nor forsake you."

I am reminded of a very familiar story in the Holy Bible in the book of Mark, Chapter 4, when Jesus and His disciples were on a ship, and Jesus had fallen asleep. A storm arose, and the winds were raging and the water began to fill the ship, and the disciples were fearful and they immediately woke up Jesus and said, "Master, cares thou not that we perish?" They thought that they were about to die.

Have you ever been in a storm in your life and you felt that death was staring you right in your face? You may have panicked. You may have cried. And you may have even said, "God, what is going on?" "Why am I feeling like I'm about to die?" "When is this storm going to end?"

You may be going through a storm right now that has yet to cease. I want you to know that you have weathered the storm long enough. The storm that you are in expires today. You are about to feel refreshed and revived, and the sun is about to shine again.

DAY SIXTEEN

I DECREE THAT I WILL OVERCOME FEAR

"Thou shalt also decree a thing, and it shall be established unto thee: and the light shall shine upon thy ways."
Job 22:28

I have learned that fear does not care who it attaches itself to. It is a weapon that the devil uses to impede anyone from moving forward. Fear will cause permanent stagnation in your life, if you allow it to.

You will never start the business if you allow fear to stick around. You will never start the ministry if you allow fear to stick around. You will never go back to school to pursue that

53

degree if you allow fear to stick around. You will never write that book if you allow fear to stick around. You will never do some of the greatest things you have always aspired to do if you allow fear to stick around. Fear is an enemy to your destiny.

I want to encourage you to make up your mind that you will not allow fear to hinder you any longer. From this day forward, you should totally have "Faith over fear."

DAY SEVENTEEN

I DECREE THAT I WILL NOT BE DEPRESSED

"Thou shalt also decree a thing, and it shall be established unto thee: and the light shall shine upon thy ways."
Job 22:28

Overdue bills, lack of finances, an unhealthy relationship or marriage, failing health, problems in the family, and problems on the job, along with so many other things, can easily make someone depressed. When the spirit of depression captures your mind, you will feel helpless and drained, and that place of isolation is where you feel most comfortable.

You may be feeling depressed right now. You may feel helpless, and you do not want to be bothered. I know how you feel because I have been there before many times. I have had those moments when I was up and those moments when I was down. There were times I felt like I was on an emotional rollercoaster. There was one particular time when I also felt like I was in a position to be defeated, because one day depression and anxiety both got the best of me. But I was determined to not allow the spirit of depression (or anxiety) to defeat me.

I have now learned to do the following things when the enemy uses situations to make me feel depressed:

I pray. I declare the peace of God over my mind. I relax, take a deep breath and softly and repeatedly say, "Jesus is Lord. Jesus is Lord. Jesus is Lord. Jesus is Lord over every situation. Jesus is Lord over my mind. Jesus is Lord over my life." As I do and say these things, I almost instantly feel better. I feel the weight of depression lifting. I encourage you to duplicate all of these things, along with some other things to include exercising to overcome depression.

DAY EIGHTEEN

I DECREE THAT I WILL HAVE SELF-CONTROL

"Thou shalt also decree a thing, and it shall be
established unto thee: and the light shall
shine upon thy ways."
Job 22:28

Have you ever responded to a situation in a way that you were not proud of? Do you often struggle with keeping your emotions under control? Do you know how to manage your actions well? Do you know how important it is for you to have self-control?

We must all learn how to have self-control. I know it may not always be an easy thing to do, especially in

59

certain situations, but it is necessary. Sometimes your emotions can get the best of you and you will find yourself doing and saying things that can create problems instead of being a solution to a problem.

If you lack self-control, you should try avoiding situations that will tempt you to react in a negative way. You should also monitor your thoughts, because the actions that you carry out will always stem from a thought. If you think positively, you will be able to respond positively to situations.

DAY NINETEEN

I DECREE THAT I WILL NOT QUIT

"Thou shalt also decree a thing, and it shall be
established unto thee: and the light shall
shine upon thy ways."
Job 22:28

You may feel the urge to quit when
things become challenging in your
life, or when you simply cannot have
your way. I want to let you know that
God did not give you the spirit to quit.
Quitting is not a part of your spiritual
DNA. Quitting is an option, but it can
no longer be your option.

You need to make up your mind
that you are not going to quit this time
around, but you are going to give it all

you got. Come hell or high water, you must be determined to stay the course and complete what you started. When you feel the urge to quit again, just repeatedly tell yourself "I can do all things through Christ who strengthens me."(Philippians 4:13). And you have to believe that you can.

DAY TWENTY

I DECREE THAT I WILL HAVE FAVOR WITH GOD AND OTHERS

"Thou shalt also decree a thing, and it shall be established unto thee: and the light shall shine upon thy ways."
Job 22:28

I am certain that you have heard people say, "Favor isn't fair." I beg to differ. I must say that favor is fair because God is the One who causes it to happen in our lives. Proverbs 3:4 NLT translation says, "You will find favor with both God and people."

It should make you feel great in knowing that God cares that much about you, that He will allow you to receive special treatment by way of

63

others showing you favor. I want to let you know that you should never find it strange when people go out of their way for you. Have you ever been in the drive through at a restaurant and the person in the car in front of yours paid for your food? Have you ever been at a grocery store and someone paid for all or some of your grocery? Has a stranger ever walked up to you and given you money or a gift? Has a coworker ever bought your lunch when you did not have any money to buy your own? Have you ever received an unexpected check in the mail? That's favor! May His favor be with you for the remainder of your life.

DAY TWENTY-ONE

I DECREE THAT I WILL MAKE BETTER DECISIONS

"Thou shalt also decree a thing, and it shall be
established unto thee: and the light shall
shine upon thy ways."
Job 22:28

All of us make decisions (good or bad) every single day, and we have to live with our decisions. Some of us have made decisions that we wish we could reverse. I wish I could reverse all the bad decisions that I ever made, but I know that is impossible. You may also feel the same way about some bad decisions you made.

Every decision comes with some form of consequence. The outcome of a bad decision is usually not good; that is why you should steer away from making bad decisions. I have learned after making so many bad decisions in my life that there is room to make better decisions. I am proud to say that I have gotten so much better. I now pray about a decision before I make it; that helps me to not get caught up in my emotions and make the wrong decision.

I encourage you to do the same. Pray about it first, and then allow God to speak to you about what you should do. When you consult God, He will always lead you the right way. He will give you peace in your spirit.

You can do better with making the right decisions, and it can start today with the one that you are about to make.

DAY TWENTY-TWO

I DECREE THAT I WILL LET GO OF THE COMPLAINING

"Thou shalt also decree a thing, and it shall be
established unto thee: and the light shall
shine upon thy ways."
Job 22:28

The Bible tells us in Philippians 2:14 to "Do everything without complaining." I have learned over the years that complaining never changes anything. That very thing that you want to complain about right now, you should be grateful that it is not worse than what it could be, "because there's someone who's worse off than you."

Someone, somewhere, does not have food to eat. Someone does not have clothes or shoes to wear. Someone does not have anywhere to stay or a bed to sleep on. Someone does not have transportation to get to their destination. Someone does not have the money to pay an overdue bill. Someone does not have enough income to even take care of their basic needs. Someone's health is failing. "There's someone else who'd love to be in your shoes" right now. So, you are encouraged to be grateful and not complain.

DAY TWENTY-THREE

I DECREE THAT I WILL OVERCOME EVIL WITH GOOD

"Thou shalt also decree a thing, and it shall be established unto thee: and the light shall shine upon thy ways."
Job 22:28

Did you know that some people are just set out to do evil? To be good to others is just far from their nature. They do not have it in their hearts to do good. Do you know some people like that? You may have some of them in your family, in your circle of so-called friends, in the workplace, and even at church.

71

You not only have to pray for people like that, you still have to treat them well. It may seem like a hard thing to do, but when you have the love of God within you, compassion will flow through you. Luke 6:27-28 says, "But to you who are listening I say: Love your enemies, do good to those who hate you, bless those who curse you, pray for those who mistreat you."

You should never be a person who desires to get even when someone intentionally mistreats you. That is not exemplifying the essence of God. You should never overcome evil with evil, but you should do as His Word instructs us to do in Roman 12:21, "…Overcome evil with good."

DAY TWENTY-FOUR

I DECREE THAT I WILL ACCEPT CHANGE

"Thou shalt also decree a thing, and it shall be
established unto thee: and the light shall
shine upon thy ways."
Job 22:28

In order to grow spiritually and explore all that God has for you, you have to be willing and ready to accept change. Of course, change is never easy for anyone. There are so many people who are set in their own ways. They have a certain mindset and dare to change it, not even slightly. They do not want to move beyond their comfort zone. They are used to doing

73

the same thing over and over again. Did you know that sometimes God will force you out of your comfort zone? Yes, even when you do not feel like moving. He knows the plan that He has for your life, and oftentimes it requires change, first in your mind.

There are some amazing things that God has for you as you go from one level to the next level, so you are encouraged to get out of your own way and allow God to bring about change in your life, as He sees fit. Change will be for your good in this season of your life.

DAY TWENTY-FIVE

I DECREE THAT I WILL NOT COMPROMISE MY VALUES

"Thou shalt also decree a thing, and it shall be established unto thee: and the light shall shine upon thy ways."
Job 22:28

You are royalty in the sight of God. You have been bought with a price. You are valuable to Him. You are also important to Him and your life matters to Him. You have to learn to see yourself as God sees you, not how other people see you.

Some people will try to minimize you and your abilities, because they only see you as an ant. They think that they are greater than you. What they

75

do not realize is that you are a giant in the world, who has the hand of God on your life, who possess so many gifts and talents, who has greatness on the inside of you. You were certified and qualified to be great the moment you were born. You have to believe that.

You must start seeing yourself as an asset and not a liability. You can no longer let people run completely over you and treat you how they want to treat you. Not in your relationship. Not in your workplace. Not in your church. Not anywhere. You have to set standards and not lower them for anyone. In order to accomplish some of the greatest things in your life, you must know your worth.

DAY TWENTY-SIX

I DECREE THAT I WILL CONNECT WITH POSITIVE, LIKE-MINDED PEOPLE

"Thou shalt also decree a thing, and it shall be established unto thee: and the light shall shine upon thy ways."
Job 22:28

When you are tired of being around people who are takers, who are secretly jealous of you, who are non-supportive, who are not moving forward or pouring into you as much as you are pouring into them, then your desire to be delivered from them and be connected to positive, like-minded people becomes great. It is so very important to God that you are

77

delivered from those people who do not mean you any good and have no intentions of ever making any positive contributions in your life.

He knows that you cannot be effective for Him if you are entangled with negative-minded people who are basically sucking the life out of you, because they do not even have what is needed to help enhance your life. They will be more of a hindrance to you than a help to you. They will even cause stagnation in your life, if you stay connected to them. You probably should be so much further on your journey, but you have been connected to the wrong people for way too long.

In this season of your life, you must be willing to let go of dead weight, that includes anything or anyone that you should not be connected to. When you release negative connections, you will be in a great position to embrace the new, positive-minded connections that God is going to send you.

DAY TWENTY-SEVEN

I DECREE THAT I WILL RECEIVE MY HEALING

"Thou shalt also decree a thing, and it shall be established unto thee: and the light shall shine upon thy ways."
Job 22:28

You may not be feeling your best right now. You may be facing an attack in every area of your life—that is, emotionally, mentally, spiritually, and physically. I know how you feel. I have been there before. I was at the brink of giving up, because I was drained in every area of my life, too, at the very same time. I want you to know that God restored and healed me, and He can do that for you, too.

81

His Word says in Isaiah 53:5, "But he was wounded for our transgressions, he was bruised for our iniquities: the chastisement of our peace was upon him; and with his stripes we are healed."

I want to encourage your heart by letting you know that God is going to touch you in a special way. He is going to heal you in whatever area of your life that it is needed. Trust Him for complete healing.

DAY TWENTY-EIGHT

I DECREE THAT I WILL
CONQUER IT

"Thou shalt also decree a thing, and it shall be
established unto thee: and the light shall
shine upon thy ways."
Job 22:28

Sometimes you can easily indulge in some things that appear to be good to and for you, but those things are designed to hinder you. Oftentimes those things will gradually become a stronghold. When something becomes a stronghold, it can and will force you into a place of spiritual stagnation. When that happens, it can impede your spiritual progress and growth.

There may be one particular thing that has caused spiritual stagnation in your life, and you really want to overcome it. I want to let you know that with God on your side, you can conquer whatever that thing is. He is about to cause that thing to loosen its grip. I am certain that you have heard, "There's nothing too hard for God." I can truly attest to that. I have learned over the years that there really isn't anything that God cannot handle. Give it to God today.

DAY TWENTY-NINE

I DECREE THAT I WILL BE PATIENT AND WAIT FOR GOD TO DO IT

"Thou shalt also decree a thing, and it shall be established unto thee: and the light shall shine upon thy ways."
Job 22:28

Some of us get in a hurry and do things our way, outside of God's timing, when it seems like what we have been praying and believing God for is taking way too long to manifest. Some of us got married outside of His timing. Some of us purchased the house and the car outside of His timing. Some of us started the ministry outside of His timing. Some of us started the business outside of His timing. Some of us have done many other things outside of His timing. It is never good to do anything outside of His timing. He has an appointed time for things to take place in our lives. All we have to do is learn how to be patient and wait on Him.

Have you ever been impatient to the point to where you did something outside of God's timing? Did you feel the stress and pain of going ahead of God instead of allowing Him to lead the way? Are you now struggling with being patient about some things that you have been praying and believing God for that has not manifested in your life? It is necessary to continue being patient, more than ever in this season of your life.

You are in your "Be Still" season. You cannot afford to be in a hurry and make another move without the lead of God. You have to learn how to be still and wait on God, despite how much you want it to happen. He knows what is best for you, so He is going to make sure whatever you have been praying and believing Him for happens in His timing. I want you to know that His timing is always perfect. "Wait on the Lord: be of good courage, and he shall strengthen thine heart: wait, I say, on the Lord." (Psalm 27:14).

DAY THIRTY

I DECREE THAT I WILL RECEIVE A BREAKTHROUGH

"Thou shalt also decree a thing, and it shall be
established unto thee: and the light shall
shine upon thy ways."
Job 22:28

God is in a position to release to
His children whatever it is we need.
He desires that we live an abundant
life and receive breakthroughs and
miracles alike. Sometimes He will
allow us to receive a breakthrough
just to show us (and even others) that
He has not forgotten about us.

I want to encourage you to continue
praying and believing God for your
breakthrough. He is honored when

89

you believe; it will make Him move suddenly for you. I must let you know that your breakthrough is going to be released sooner than later. It is closer than you can imagine.

DECREE IT AND LET GOD MANIFEST IT

_____

_____

_____

_____

_____

_____

_____

_____

_____

_____

_____

_____

_____

_____

_____

_____

DECREE IT AND LET GOD MANIFEST IT

_____

_____

_____

_____

_____

_____

_____

_____

_____

_____

_____

_____

_____

_____

DECREE IT AND LET GOD MANIFEST IT

_____

_____

_____

_____

_____

_____

_____

_____

_____

_____

_____

_____

_____

_____

_____

DECREE IT AND LET GOD MANIFEST IT

_____

_____

_____

_____

_____

_____

_____

_____

_____

_____

_____

_____

_____

_____

_____

_____

_____

DECREE IT AND LET GOD MANIFEST IT

_____

_____

_____

_____

_____

_____

_____

_____

_____

_____

_____

_____

_____

_____

_____

_____

DECREE IT AND LET GOD MANIFEST IT

_____

_____

_____

_____

_____

_____

_____

_____

_____

_____

_____

_____

_____

_____

_____

_____

_____

DECREE IT AND LET GOD MANIFEST IT

_____

_____

_____

_____

_____

_____

_____

_____

_____

_____

_____

_____

_____

_____

_____

_____

_____

DECREE IT AND LET GOD MANIFEST IT

_____

_____

_____

_____

_____

_____

_____

_____

_____

_____

_____

_____

_____

_____

_____

_____

DECREE IT AND LET GOD MANIFEST IT

_____

_____

_____

_____

_____

_____

_____

_____

_____

_____

_____

_____

_____

_____

_____

_____

_____

DECREE IT AND LET GOD MANIFEST IT

If you enjoyed reading this book, you may love reading Yolanda's other books. Here are the titles of her other books and they can be found on the following sites:

www.amazon.com
www.barnesandnoble.com
www.booksamillion.com

1. From Victim to Virtuous for Women
2. From Victim to Virtuous for Little Girls
3. From Victim to Virtuous for Teen Girls
4. From Rejection to Relationship with God

5. A Word for Your Mind, Spirit and Soul for Everyday of the Year (Daily Devotional)
6. A Virtuous Woman's Prayer is Jesus, Fill My Cup! (Weekly Devotional)
7. I Am Pretty Enough (version for girls)
8. I Am Pretty Enough (version for women)
9. I Am Worthy Enough

The fourth and fifth book listed are for both women and men.